THE PUPPY

Artlist Collection

THE ORIGINAL · ACCEPT NO COPYCATS

THE DOG
Artlist Collection

CARLTON
BOOKS

Introduction

The cute stranger is at first slightly unsure, a little hesitant, but you know you've made a special connection from the very moment your eyes first meet. The first uncertain steps turn into a headlong rush and there is an enchanting sparkle in the stranger's clear, dark eyes as he falls into your arms for your first kiss. He sticks his cold wet nose in your ear and scrapes his gooey tongue up the side of your face. It's love at first sight. It's puppy love!

Who can resist the unbridled affections of a puppy? You'd have to be the most cold-hearted person in the world, or possibly a cat. The images presented in *The Puppy* show the most adorable, lovable puppies you are ever likely to see. Following the success of its parent book, *The Dog*, *The Puppy* collection uses the same 'Strange Ratio' photography that made *The Dog* not only a delightful book, but also one of the most prolific ranges of licensed product to emerge from Japan in recent years, the merchandise encompassing everything from T-shirts and backpacks to bedspreads and coffee mugs.

The 'Strange Ratio' technique exaggerates that part of the puppy that is closest to the camera – usually, but not always, its head. This makes it look just like the little mites are about to launch themselves at you, so brace yourselves because a happy puppy only knows one way to share his happiness – it's high energy, it's sloppy and it's in your face!

THIS IS A CARLTON BOOK

The Dog Logo and Photographs © 2004
Artlist International Inc
Design copyright © 2005
Carlton Books Limited
Text copyright © 2005 Rod Green

This edition published in 2005 by
Carlton Books Ltd
A Division of the Carlton Publishing Group
20 Mortimer Street
London
W1T 3JW

A CIP catalogue for this book is available
from the British Library.

ISBN 1 84442 479 0

Executive Editor: Amie McKee
Art Director: Clare Baggaley
Senior Art Editor: Zoë Dissell
Design: Stuart Smith
Production: Lisa Moore

Printed and bound in Dubai

 # Contents

Golden Retriever

I just can't decide what to do when I grow up. Golden Retrievers can do so many things. I could work as a gun dog, which is the job dogs like me always used to do; or I could work as a guide dog with blind people; I could be a sniffer dog, helping the police to find drugs or explosives, or I could work as a search-and-rescue dog. That's the trouble with coming from such a clever family – we're good at so many things. Maybe someone will want me as a family pet. I love playing with children and I'm very easy to train, but I like to be active, so I need lots of long walks. Well, no point in worrying. I'll concentrate on being a puppy for a while longer!

🦴 *Which one do you think I should have on my passport?*

♪ *You have to concentrate hard to catch a bluebottle …*

Basset Hound

I tripped over my own ear again this morning. One second I was running like a train, the next I was doing somersaults. We all laughed about it, but I made sure I didn't lose the smell I was chasing. Smells are the best things ever! I've got a great nose for sniffing out really snuffly whiffs and that's what I like doing best. This morning it was the whiff of a chubby-mushy-chewy-tingly-juicy thing. I followed that whiff for miles, but I never caught up with it. Don't know what I'd do if I did – howl at it, probably. That's the other thing I'm really good at – chasing whiffs and howling. Once I'm bigger, I'll let out a proper howl that'll be so loud you'll wish you had ear flaps like mine!

♪ Look into my eyes … you want to go for a walk in the park …
you really, really want to go for a walk in the park …

15

American Cocker Spaniel

I think it's time for another run in the park. What do you mean we only got back five minutes ago? Five minutes is a long time, isn't it? Seems like ages to me. I like running around and bouncing about and chasing my ball and dashing and dodging and galloping and jumping. We can't do that sitting here, can we? Oh, you're not going to brush my ears again, are you? I have to sit still for that and you know I hate sitting still. You'll give me a treat if I sit still? And you're going to brush the whole lot? But we did that yesterday – or was it the day before? Never mind, I'll sit still. I'm ready for the treat. My mouth's watering, but I'm sitting totally still – almost. It is okay if I wag my tail, isn't it?

♪ I think she's looking at our leads.
We're going for a walk!

♪ Is she really? Are you sure?

17

♪ Oooh – I can't bear to look.

19

♪ *Don't you just hate it when you wake up from a nap and someone's sleeping on your ear?*

Miniature Pinscher

Don't laugh. She's feeling a bit sad. She just found out that she'll never grow up to be a Dobermann Pinscher. We're not even closely related to Dobermanns, but who cares really? They may be several times our size but they're not even half as good looking as us – and we're far more practical, especially if you live in a smaller house or an apartment. We don't take up as much room as a Dobermann would – you'd need a house the size of an aircraft hangar for those guys. We won't hog the sofa and we don't eat as much as Dobermanns, but we do make terrific guard dogs. We like plenty of walks to keep us in shape, but that's good for you, too. So why would you want a Dobermann when you could have us?

20

♪ *Don't yell at him. He didn't mean to knock the plant over.*

♪ *Now you've really upset him.*

♪ *She'll never reach it in time …*

23

♪ *Ooooh … what a backhand return! We love watching tennis on TV.*

Chihuahua

I think that being small is really cool. 'The best things come in small packages' is what people say, and as far as dog packages go, we Chihuahuas are pretty much as small as they come. Our name is also totally cool – a big name for little guys – Chihuahua. It's Mexican and you have to say it 'Chee-waa-waa'. I can say my name, and that's something most big dogs can't do. Try getting a German Shepherd Dog to say its name – and then try lifting it into your car using only one hand. Yup, being small is pretty cool.

✔ Get off! For the last time – I am not a motorbike!

✔ We are Chihuahuas not Yamahas.

27

♪ *The one with the stupid jumper on says I look like a badger!*
I don't, do I?

Bulldog

Are you sure this is my coat and not my big brother's? I know I'm going to have lots of muscles and big, broad shoulders like my dad one day, but how am I supposed to practise acting like a tough guy when I keep tripping over my own face? Dad's not as tough as he looks, either. He likes playing with children and napping on the couch, just like I do. He's not as fluffy and soft as me, though, so I get more cuddles than he does. I suppose that's one good thing about having to wear a coat that's ten sizes too big for you!

♪ *Is it just my imagination, or do I really look like a pyjama case from behind?*

29

♪ *The problem with taking so many naps is that we always look as though we've just woken up!*

It always makes me smile when people slip in a pool of my drool.

33

♪ *I'm scared that if I run too fast and stop suddenly, my coat will fall forward over my head.*

Pekingese

Peking is in China, you know. At least, it used to be. They call it something different now – Beijing. I'm glad we came from China a long time ago. I wouldn't like to be called Beijingese. That would make me really grumpy, and I don't need any more help with my grumpiness, thank you very much. I like to be given attention when I want it and to be left alone when I don't want it. I don't like noisy children poking and prodding me, and I don't like it if you leave it too long before brushing me. Those are my rules. Stick to my rules and I'll be your best friend forever. Otherwise, I'll be like a (rather small) bear with a sore head.

♪ We're not all grumpy, you know. I just
wagged my tail so hard it knocked me over!

35

Jack Russell Terrier

There are so many things you don't know when you're as small as me. I don't know if I'm going to have a neat, smooth coat or a rough, fluffy one. I don't know if I'm going to have to go out chasing rats and things on a farm or if I'll be kept safe at home as a pet. I know I don't like being stuck in a house all day, though. I need to run around outside a lot. That's what I like to do best – run and chase things. I'm really good at chasing pigeons. I've never caught one, though. Do you think if I did he'd stay and play instead of flying away. I hate it when they do that. How do they manage it, anyway? See? There's another thing I just don't know.

♪ My patch is on my left eye and I like my ears down ...

♪ My patch is on the right and I like my ears up. Now can you tell us apart?

🦴 *How come my back end always wakes up first after a nap?*

40

… and if you don't say sorry about eating his lunch, he's never going to speak to you again.

41

Dandie Dinmont Terrier

Why on earth should anyone think that I would want to have lovely, smooth, silky hair growing on my head? I'm scruffy. It's just the way I am, and I'm happy with it. Being scruffy is the way you need to be when you like wrestling and digging and getting mucky like I do. What do I want with a posh haircut? Well I'm not having it. You can't make me do something once my mind is made up, and I've decided – if I can't stay scruffy then I'm just not going to grow up. Growing up is no fun – I'm staying a puppy.

43

♪ *What do you mean,
'Punk Rock's not cool any more'?*

Polish Lowland Sheepdog

Sorry I'm late. I was just rounding up some
stray toys in the garden. I had to do a lot of
running but I did get them all into a nice neat
pile. Maybe one day they will let me round up
some sheep. I'm pretty good at rounding up
children, too. I love playing with kids and they
love tickling me because I have such long,
fluffy hair. It will get longer as I grow and it'll
need lots of brushing, but it does keep me
really warm. That's good because I like to be
outside as much as possible. Can I go and
check on those toys again, please?

✔ *That's not my best side, you know.*

49

♪ *There, that's better, isn't it?*

Saluki

Look how long my legs are. You can tell I'm going to be tall, can't you? I'm going to be tall and a very fast runner. I was running so fast this morning, I thought I was going to take off. If only I could flap my ears like wings! Then somebody banged a truck door shut and I got such a fright I nearly jumped out of my skin. I don't really like loud noises – they make me nervous. I needed a big hug to calm me down. Make hugs, not bangs – that's what I say.

 I may have a nap now. Keep the noise down, please.

51

Saint Bernard

Take a look at me in these pictures and I'll show you why Saint Bernards are the most famous mountain-rescue dogs in the world. First of all you can see me flying along like 'Superdog to the rescue!' Looks like I'm snoozing? Yeah, you're right. We don't do flying. We are among the biggest dogs around, though, so we like to do a lot of bounding and lolloping. Also, check out under my chin – that's where we carry little brandy kegs for people stranded in the snow. Not there is it? Despite the stories, we don't do that, either. Brandy would be really bad for someone needing to be rescued. What we are really famous for is being big and strong and gentle – so how about a tickle?

52

53

♪ Why don't you pick me up for a cuddle
before I get too big?

So when you're taking photos, you only use one eye, like this?

Lakeland Terrier

What does that camera thing do then? Can I play with it? Is it good to chew? Can I have a go? I'm pretty smart, you know. I figured out how to open the fridge yesterday. Lakelands like me are well known for being clever – and a bit cheeky. Do you think I'm cheeky? I can't help it – I just like to be the centre of attention most of the time. Okay … all of the time. Surely I deserve a bit of fuss, though. After all, I do keep the children amused and, even though I won't grow very big, I am a great watchdog. Now, are you going to let me have a go with that thing, or not?

55

Japanese Spitz

It's not easy being so white, you know. All I have to do is step outside and I seem to get covered in mud every time. I can't help dashing around a lot. You have to dash around to catch balls and frisbees and that's what I like doing. Nobody seems to mind if I get a bit mucky, though. They just give me a good brush. When I'm bigger, my coat will be longer and I'll need a lot more brushing, but I'm still going to run around a lot. I need to stay really fit, you see, to make sure I can guard the house. I may not grow very big, but I'd never let a stranger near. If I hear someone at the front door, I bark like mad and run everywhere. I'm as fast as lightning. Maybe that's why I'm so white.

🦴

57

♪ *Just ignore him. We've been out in the rain.*
He thinks he's my hair dryer.

Doberman

Some say we're the most feared dogs on the planet. They say we're really scary, vicious guard dogs. I ask you, do I look that scary to you? Do I look vicious? My dad was playing with me and some children in the garden a few minutes ago. He was taller than most of them, but he was very gentle with them. He even licked them. I did, too. Now you might think that, as it was getting close to dinner time, we were just finding out which one tasted best – we do need big meals, after all. But we wouldn't eat children – they smell disgusting!

🦴 The best thing to do after lunch is have a snooze
and dream about dinner.

French Bulldog

Do you see these ears? That's what makes me different from an English Bulldog. We French Bulldogs have fantastic, pointy ears, not like those folded-over, floppy English Bulldog ones. Also, even though I will be smaller than an English Bulldog when I'm fully grown, my coat will fit better and my face won't look as though I'd just run into the back of a big red London Bus. It's all a matter of style, you see. We French Bulldogs have style from the tops of our ears to the tips of our tails. My tail wags all the time. You don't think it spoils my image, do you?

61

♪ *I think this is going to be a bit of a 'tongue out' day.*

♪ *Just take the photo and get me off this chair!*

63

Irish Setter

Were you thinking of going out somewhere?
For a walk maybe? A run would be even
better! I'll race you ten times round the park
and you have to leap over that bench beside
the pond every lap. If I win, I get to eat your
dinner. If you win, you can have mine. You
don't fancy mine? Okay, I'll have both. No
deal? Can we run anyway? Sitting around
here isn't much fun, I need to get out. If I'm
awake, I need to be doing something. You
think I look beautiful? Okay, just a couple more
photographs, but then we can go out, right?
Okay, it's a deal. Does the deal still include
your dinner? No? Pity.

♪ *If this was a mirror, you would be as beautiful as me!*

Akita

Is it time for me to be brushed again yet? I love being brushed – it's tickly and it makes my coat shine. If I'm not going to be brushed, then how about some lunch? I need plenty of food to build up my muscles. You might think that because my family is Japanese I'll always be quite small, but when I grow up I'm going to be as big as a German Shepherd and just as smart. But I'm not going to put up with hordes of kids pulling my tail or trying to ride on my back like I'm some kind of soppy Labrador. No way! Okay, maybe I'd like a bit of a pat now and again, or a good brush. That reminds me – where's my lunch?

♪ *The trouble with having a tail that curls over is that I keep thinking I'm being followed!*

67

♪ *Okay, from down there maybe I do look like a walking head.*

Cavalier King Charles Spaniel

If I am King Charles, then shouldn't you give
me a bow? No, not a 'bow-wow', just a bow,
or a curtsy if you prefer, or that treat I can
smell in your pocket, maybe? I've got a pretty
good sense of smell, you know, even though
I'm not a tracker or a hunter or any kind of
working dog. We Cavaliers have never
needed to work. Our only job has been
keeping people company, just as our ancestors
long ago kept King Charles II company. Our
long ears even look a bit like his long hair,
although I shouldn't think his hair trailed
along the ground the way my ears sometimes
do. I can keep you company now, if you like.
How about that treat, then?

71

🦴 *Actually, I think this is my best side …*

74

🦴 *They found us! How did they guess we were hiding under the rug?*

Chow Chow

So what if I look like a pile of fluff that a breeze just blew out from under the bed? My fur coat is brilliant for keeping me cosy on cold days in the park and in a couple of months I'm going to be so strong and tough that even a hurricane couldn't shift me, never mind a breeze. I hate it when it gets too hot, though, especially in a warm house. People shouldn't keep their houses too hot – they should just grow fur coats like mine. Now where did you go? Over there? I can't really see that well from under all this fur!

76

✦ You know, sometimes I wonder if I've got my head on the right way up.

Boston Terrier

I come from Boston, Massachusetts, in the
United States. We Boston Terriers are proud to
be one of the oldest American breeds. Some
people even like to call us the National Dog of
America. We don't fight or chase rats like
ordinary terriers – we're much too smart for
that. And since we are the National Dog, I
have decided that when I grow up I am going
to become President. The first thing I'm going
to do when I am President is get myself some
ears that fit properly. Well, you don't expect
the President's ears to start flapping in a
breeze, do you?

♪ *Hurry up, fetch a lead! The future President of the United States needs to go walkies!*

81

Maltese

I'm never going to be able to cope with this hair. Every day is a bad hair day for me. It's okay for my mum. She just wafts along in her long, flowing coat like she's floating on air. I blow into the room like a snowdrift. She may not be tall, but she crosses the room like a supermodel. I cross the room like a floor duster. You think my coat looks cute? Really? And I'll have a coat just like my mum when I'm bigger. She has to be brushed every day, you know. I think I'll quite like that. I'd much rather be a supermodel than a snowdrift.

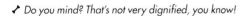
✦ *Do you mind? That's not very dignified, you know!*

♪ *She says she's not going to sit up for a photo until whoever took the squeaky bone chew she got for her birthday owns up.*

84

♪ *I didn't take it! And I didn't hide it in my basket under the blanket beside the floppy bunny while everyone was having lunch, either!*

🦴 *This is the paw that stood in chewing gum and got me stuck to the pavement!*

Dalmatian

Look at all my lovely spots! Aren't they beautiful? I've not had them for very long, you know. When I was really tiny I was pure white – not a spot in sight. Then, when I was about three weeks old, they started to appear. Now I've got hundreds. You should see them when I'm running. My legs are getting so long now that I can run like the wind. I can get up such a speed that I'm just a blur and my spots are more like stripes. Dalmatians like me have always been fast runners. People used to use us to chase after animals they were hunting and they also liked us to run alongside old-fashioned horse-drawn carriages or even fire engines. Sounds great to me!

♪ Quick – check the floor. I think one of my spots fell off!

Tibetan Spaniel

Go on, be honest. You don't think I'm a cat, do you? They say I'm like a cat because I like climbing and sitting on things high up. That's not because I'm like a cat, though, it's because I come from the mountains in Tibet where we were watchdogs in monasteries. We used to sit on the monastery walls to warn the monks when strangers approached, so we're happy up high. And even though I don't grow very big, I'll still be bigger than most cats. I can bark, too, not meow like a cat. Anyway, my job is to be your friend, playmate and watchdog. Who ever heard of a watch cat?

♪ *We only wanted to climb up on the shelf. We didn't know ornaments could fall and break into tiny pieces!*

Wire Fox Terrier

Come on, let's play! I know you've nothing better to do. How could you not want to play? Let's go looking for rats and mice then. You want to stay indoors? Okay, I don't mind being indoors for a while. Come on, let's play! Did I just say that? It's a good idea, though. Oh, don't bother brushing me – my coat's wiry, so I don't need brushing often. I need to be played with, though. You're expecting someone to call round? That's okay – I'll bark if anyone comes near the house. You know I always do. Shall I fetch my ball now?

🦴 ... and that's how I keep my whiskers fluffed up.

Labrador Retriever

Do you mind? I'm trying to have a nap. Don't worry, I still love you. How do I know I love you? Hey, I'm a Labrador – I love everybody! When I grow up I'm going to be a guide dog, helping blind people. I like to help out. You can rely on me. I'll happily play with the children for hours. That's why I'm feeling so sleepy now. I've been running about and playing for ages and then I had a huge dinner. I would eat until I burst if you let me. Those are all the things I like – being lovable, helping, playing, running, eating … and there was one more thing. Ah, yes … sleeping. Goodnight!

♪ Mmmmmmm … it's that 'Mountain of Dog Biscuits' dream again …

♪ *We love fetching things. We'll fetch anything you want. You name it, we'll fetch it. Nothing? Okay, how about a hug, then?*

♪ *Nope – I've looked all around down here and I still can't see what you're standing on.*

Dachshund

Ah … a nice long nap is exactly what a nice long dog like me needs. Actually, I'm not really very long, I'm just low. I only have little short legs, you see, so I look like I'm even longer and lower than I really am. That's why people sometimes call me a 'sausage dog' – because they think I'm shaped like a sausage. I don't mind. I love running around and playing but it is exhausting when you have such short legs. Even when I'm older my legs won't get much longer, but I think that's just as well, really. Short legs leave me closer to the ground and that's very handy for when you suddenly need an emergency nap!

♪ *I'm sure I left my woolly toy over here …*

♪ *Hee-hee!*

♪ Ha-ha! He's so funny when he pretends to go surfing!

♪ *Don't know why I stole this – it tastes horrible!*

Newfoundland

You probably think I look really adorable.
That's because I am. You probably also want
to give me a big hug and take me home with
you. Well, I like hugs, but unless you live in a
large house near the sea or a lake, then I
won't be happy living with you. I'm going to
be pretty big when I grow up. Huge, in fact.
And I'll need a lot of space and I'll need to go
swimming. We Newfoundlands are water
dogs, you see. We used to help fishermen with
their nets and now we work as search-and-
rescue dogs in coastal areas. We do need a
bit of persuading to get us going, though,
because we can sometimes be a little bit lazy.
Well, when you're a big as we are, you need
to save as much energy as you can just for
wagging your tail!

🦴 *We're not lazy. Standing up is just a bit of an effort, that's all!*

Beagle

Do you like playing? I do! I like rolling and
wrestling and chasing and jumping and
tumbling and spinning round and round. I get
really sad if I'm ever on my own – I like it best
when there are lots of children or other dogs to
play with. Then we can go out in the garden or
to the park and even if I get a bit dirty or
muddy it doesn't really matter because my
short coat is pretty much wipe-clean. They say I
might work as a sniffer dog for the customs
men when I grow up, helping them to find stuff
that's being smuggled in people's baggage or
maybe even explosives. I'd like that. It sounds
like a great game to play.

♪ Help me! I'm a midget trapped inside a Beagle fancy dress outfit!

♪ He's always trying that one, but they still never let him on the sofa.

♪ *You put your left ear in, your left ear out …*

♪ … In-out, in-out, shake it all about …

♪ He's sulking because you made him get out of the dirty washing basket.

109

Flat-Coated Retriever

Boy, am I happy! Sometimes I'm so happy my tail goes like a propeller all day long. I'm especially happy when I'm outside running around, playing fetch and splashing in water. That's what Retrievers always do best, of course, fetch things. We've always been used for fetching ducks and other birds that have been shot by hunters, you see. If the poor old duck lands in the water, so much the better – we get to fetch and splash. I'm not sure I would be quite so happy living in a house in the middle of a big town, though. I do like a lot of open space. I suppose it would be okay as long as I got loads of love and attention and exercise. Then I'd be happy. Uh-oh … there goes the tail again!

♪ …and they fill up this thing called a bath with warm water and just lie in it! I've seen them do it!

111

♪ Brilliant! When can we have a go?

🦴 *Ouch!*

🦴 *Shiny floors can do that to you sometimes.*

The answer to the shiny floor problem is to run really fast and go …

… Wheeeeeeeeeeeeeeee!

113

Siberian Husky

Everybody seems to think that all Huskies can do is pull sledges. Not me – I've never even seen snow. I bet it would be great for digging in, though. I love digging. I dug three huge holes in the garden today – one was so big that I thought I was going to fall in. I'd like to have a go at the sledge thing because I like exploring, you see. Also, when I'm bigger I will have a really thick coat that would keep me warm in the snow. They say that when I get my coat the whole house will be covered in hairs. They'd better not moan at me about that, though, or I might just give them one of my famous, extra-long, extra-loud howls. You can't beat a good howl.

116

*♪ I don't know why everyone should be so grumpy with us
just because we howled all night.*

✦ There it is! Can you see it!

✦ It moves really fast.

West Highland White Terrier

This is the way we Westies most like to spend the day – all together. We love being part of a family and we can't stand being on our own. If we're left alone, we get very bored, you see, so we have to keep ourselves amused by digging holes in things or chewing stuff. And it's not because we're only puppies – grown-up Westies get just as bored. I suppose older Westies are still a bit like puppies. We all love to run and play and we always want everybody to be having fun. That's why we need you around all the time – so that we can make sure you're enjoying yourself!

♪ Oh, for goodness sake! It's only an ant!

119

♪ It's a bit scary!

🦴 *We're settling down for a nap, but you can still wake us if you're going out to play, okay?*

121

♪ *Keep an eye on that ant, boys, don't lose sight of it!*

♪ *What exactly is an ant?*

♪ Your mother's sister! Ha-ha!

Pembroke Welsh Corgi

I know that we're going to grow a bit bigger as we get older, but we're never going to be huge, are we? I mean, we're never going to be the size of a cow. So how come they used to use us for herding cattle? I've seen a cow and it was massive. How on earth is a little thing like me supposed to be able to tell them what to do? I don't think I'd like that. What I like is when people make a fuss of me. Everybody loves us, especially the Queen. We're her favourites. We're Royal Dogs – far too good to be chasing cows.

♪ *I'm practising bowing in case the Queen drops by.*

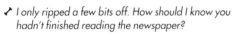 *I only ripped a few bits off. How should I know you hadn't finished reading the newspaper?*

127

♪ *Chaa! I think I got a bit of the TV guide stuck in my throat.*

Bernese Mountain Dog

See what it says? Bernese Mountain Dog – bet you thought we were Saint Bernards, didn't you? Lots of people get us mixed up but you shouldn't. We both come from Switzerland, but they have more orangey-red bits and we have more black bits, and when they grow up they're much bigger than us. When we're older we're going to be huge – like a small horse, I heard someone say. But Saint Bernards are even bigger – probably about the size of a house, I think. Can we go outside now? We don't really like being indoors. We want to practise barking. We heard our dad bark once and we thought it was an earthquake! It was brilliant! We just sound like ants with hiccups. Can we go now, please?

128

♪ *Cover your ears! He's practising the big bark again!*

✦ This is what I like to call my Swiss Roll.

Shiba Inu

I managed to sneak out of the garden again this morning. I squeezed through a hole in the fence. Everybody rushed out to bring me back, otherwise I could have escaped completely. I know it's a bit naughty, but I can't help it. I just love to go exploring, and I wanted to see where that other dog was going when he came walking past. I'm not very keen on other dogs. When I'm bigger I'll chase them away from our house. I'll be a bit too big for squeezing through gaps then, but I've been practising jumping. In a few months time I'll be able to leap clean over the fence. Then that other dog will be in for a surprise!

♪ *They're practising for the Canine Olympics.*
They're the Shiba Inu Formation Snooze Team.

135

🦴 *They all think it's funny, but I just can't keep all my paws under control on a polished floor!*

137

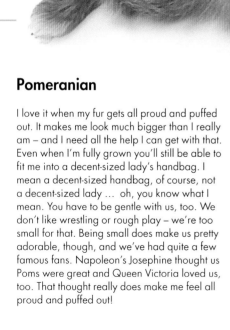

Pomeranian

I love it when my fur gets all proud and puffed out. It makes me look much bigger than I really am – and I need all the help I can get with that. Even when I'm fully grown you'll still be able to fit me into a decent-sized lady's handbag. I mean a decent-sized handbag, of course, not a decent-sized lady … oh, you know what I mean. You have to be gentle with us, too. We don't like wrestling or rough play – we're too small for that. Being small does make us pretty adorable, though, and we've had quite a few famous fans. Napoleon's Josephine thought us Poms were great and Queen Victoria loved us, too. That thought really does make me feel all proud and puffed out!

✦ *Is this a cute enough pose for you?*

✔ *Oh, not another photo! I'm getting cross now.*

141

Yorkshire Terrier

When you see all of the different colours in my coat – gold, red, grey, blue, even some highlights that look pure white – it's hard to believe that when I was born a few weeks ago, I was completely black. I looked like a little sooty rag. I much prefer having all of these lovely colours – they're going to look great in a few months time when my hair grows longer. I will still be quite small, but I'll need to be brushed a lot. I'm looking forward to that, as long as I'm allowed to go crazy afterwards and get all messed up again!

♪ *I think we're colourful enough without the brown and white stripes, don't you?*

143

Boxer

I'm not fierce, honestly. I like to be patted and I like to play. Just because I'm called a Boxer and I'm going to grow up big and muscley doesn't mean I want to fight all the time. They do say we were called Boxers because we used to stand on our back legs and swipe with our front paws when we were forced to fight long ago. We don't fight any more, though. We are very law-abiding. In fact, some of my relatives are Police Dogs. So if you don't give me a hug, I might just have you arrested!

🦴

♪ *With two sets of legs to cross, I can sit twice as comfortably as you can!*

Border Collie

The little girl I met today is quite nice, I suppose, but I like her dad better. I heard him say that Border Collies are the hardest-working, quickest-thinking, most agile of all dogs. He said we are brave and loyal, love to be trained because we are so intelligent and inquisitive, and can easily learn to understand commands, even if they are given as whistles, which is how Collies help to herd sheep. He thought we were the best of all dogs – energetic, with the stamina to run for miles every day and an unbeatable talent for problem solving. Simply the best. Real heroes. Top dogs. So why does the kid want to call me Fluffy Tum?

♪ *Isn't it my turn to take a few pictures yet?*

150

Leonberger

If you think I look big as a puppy, you wait 'til you see me when I've grown up. I'm going to be one of the biggest dogs around – almost as big as a Great Dane. I suppose some people might be a bit scared of me, but I'll always be kind and gentle. Once they get used to how big we are, children love us, especially because we like to play a lot. We're not the kind of big dog that likes to lie around all day. We like bounding around the garden and digging enormous holes – and that makes us very hungry. We like to eat a lot. In fact, I'd like to eat now. Too early for lunch? How about a snack then? Elevenses?

🦴 Hey! I'm awake. That means I should be either eating or
playing, so how about a nice big bowlful?

English Cocker Spaniel

Some people say I'm a bit crazy because I have so much energy and dash around all the time, but I'm not crazy, I just like having fun! I love to learn new tricks and games and some of my cousins work as gun dogs, retrieving small birds. I'm just as happy as a family pet, although I will grow to be slightly bigger than my relatives, the American Cocker Spaniels. I love to be the centre of attention and having someone to play with. And I like to be given a good brush because that stops me from getting nasty tangled bits, especially in my ears. It's worth the effort because I am so much fun!

🦴 *Please come and play … I'll give you a big lick!*

155

156

♪ *Are you finished yet? Is it over? Can we go? If we have to sit still a moment longer we're going to explode!*

Bichon Frisé

You won't leave me alone, will you? I get really fretful on my own. I like being around people, you see. I'm very good company. I like to listen to all your problems and give you lots of affection. All I really need in return is to be brushed every day – which makes me feel nice for you to pat – and a short walk now and again. I'm happy living in a small house or an apartment as long as you're around, and I don't get very big so I don't eat much. So you won't leave me all on my own, will you?

Rottweiler

Nice camera. You wouldn't want anyone to steal it, would you? I can guard it for you, if you like. I'm pretty strong, even for a puppy. You wait till I'm fully grown, though. I'm going to be really big with lots of muscles. That's why we Rottweilers make such good guard dogs. Nobody will try to steal anything from you if they have to get past one of us first. We are tough dogs and very serious about our jobs. All we ask in return is a little attention from our boss and a mountain of food every day. So would you like me to guard your camera? No? How about a mountain of food anyway?

♪ Halt! Who goes there?

Shih Tzu

Pretty good roar, isn't it? That's because it's my lion impression. Shih Tzus are also known as Lion Dogs, because that's what our name means in Chinese. I wonder why they called us that? Maybe it's because we grow really long hair, like a lion's mane, when we're older. It's certainly not because we're as big as lions. We're really quite small – only about the size of a lion's paw, in fact! They also call us Chrysanthemum Dogs after the flower because of the way our hair 'flowers' around our faces. Who wants to be a flower, though? I'd much rather be a lion!

162

♪ *What on earth is that thing?*

♪ *It's either a Saint Bernard … or a sofa.*

164

♪ Hey, where do you think this trail of crumbs leads?

Pug

Yaaaaah! That's what one of my yawns sounds like. Now can you tell me what it looks like? I've never seen it. Every time it happens my eyes shut. I like a good yawn and a stretch – it helps me to build up my muscles. My mum and dad are really strong, even though they're not very big. We've never really needed to grow bigger, you see. Our job has always been to hang around the house as pets and we're really good at it. We should be. We've been doing it for more than 1,000 years – since the days when we were kept as palace dogs in China, in fact. Ooooo ... here comes another yawn. Must be time for a quick nap. Cover your ears, though – we pugs are famous for our snoring!

♪ *Your breath really is bad. Look – he's fainted!*

167

♪ It looks silly? So how do you get food off your nose, then?

Airedale Terrier

Don't think that because I'm a terrier, I'm going to grow up to be a small dog. I'm going to be as big as a Labrador, but not quite as stocky. I'll have longer legs and neck than a Lab, but not such a sturdy body. Of course, we look nothing like each other. Labs don't have fantastic wiry hair like mine and I'm going to grow a beard, whether it's fashionable or not. You'll never see a soppy Labrador with a beard, will you? I'm fun to have around the family and I make a good guard dog but I need to run a lot to keep fit. Think you could keep up with me. I bet my beard you couldn't!

Afghan Hound

When you're a puppy like me with short legs and short hair, it's hard to imagine being tall and elegant with lots of lovely long hair. Everyone says how beautiful our mum is, but they just call us 'cute'. Mum spends hours every week being brushed – she has to be brushed every day to keep her coat shiny and to stop horrible thick matted bits forming. I don't think I want to be brushed that much. I quite like being small with short hair. We're beautiful too, aren't we?

✔ *This is how I practise being tall.*

173

Bouvier des Flandres

I've heard that they make delicious chocolate in Belgium. That's where I come from – Belgium – but I've no idea what chocolate tastes like. I'm not allowed to eat any because it wouldn't be good for me. I eat plenty of proper food, though, to help me grow big. When I'm older I'm going to be very tall and strong. We Bouviers used to work as cattle herders, but now we're more likely to be police dogs. Maybe if I arrested a chocolate I might get to find out what it tastes like!

♪ He says he's my friend, so why won't he share those biscuits he's hiding?

175

Shetland Sheepdog

I can't believe this lot have all fallen asleep. Didn't they realise they were about to have their photo taken? It's a bit embarrassing, really. Shetland Sheepdogs like us are known for being bright and alert. Maybe they just got a bit warm and dozy now that our big thick coats are starting to grow. You think they're sleeping off their lunch? You gave them lunch? What about me? You gave me lunch, too? When was that? I see … just before I fell asleep. Well, if I'm awake, they should be, too. I'll give them an alarm bark. That's another thing we're famous for – we're great barkers. Come on, then! Wakey-wakey!

177

... and if I open this wide, you can see all the way down to my tail!

♪ I'm sure I had one more dog biscuit left to eat here ...

♪ Don't tell her – I've got my paw on it!

Miniature Schnauzer

Miniature? Pah! There's nothing miniature about our moustaches, that's for sure. Look at them bristling out in fine style … and we're not even teenagers yet. We're very proud of our moustaches, and the rest of our hairy coats. We grow hair so fast that we could be baldies at breakfast and a heavy-metal band by teatime. We need lots of grooming and proper trimming, but if you think we're hairy, you should see our cousins, the Giant Schnauzers. Now that's what I call whiskers.

♪ I know it looks disgusting but it's the only way
to keep your moustache fluffed up.

♪ Look at him! The silly fool thinks the woollen bone is real!

183

♪ Yeah … silly fool … Wish I had one …

Poodle

It's a funny name, isn't it? 'Poodle' sounds a bit silly, in fact. But I'm not silly – I'm really clever. I even know what Poodle means. You might think it sounds a bit like puddle, and it does, because it comes from a German word, pudeln, which means to splash about. Apparently, we used to live in marshes, where we would splash around helping to hunt for ducks. I heard all about it while I was being dried off after jumping in the pond in the park. I got into big trouble for that but I just couldn't help it. I was only poodling!

🦴 I love his bedtime stories.

185

🦴 … and then the big, brown bear
came stomping out of the woods …

Old English Sheepdog

How can I be an Old English Sheepdog when I was only born a couple of months ago? I mean, my big, fluffy, grown-up, long coat has only just started to appear and I still feel very young. I'm not sure that will ever change, though. I think dogs like me will always be young at heart and playful. I love joining in all the fun and games with the children in our family and they look after me really well, brushing me and taking me for lots of walks. I'm going to grow quite big, so I'll need lots of walks. That's something I'll always want to do – even when I am old!

187

♪ *Is it true we're going to grow even more hair? We can hardly see past our own noses as it is!*

189

German Shepherd

I may be small now, but when I'm big I'm going to be a police dog. At the moment I'm not too keen on strangers, loud bangs, being on my own, cars, trucks, buses, aeroplanes, frisbees (one got me on the nose last week) or even that stupid washing machine thing in the kitchen – but when I'm big I'll be fearless. My mum is really clever and knows how to do all sorts of smart things. She's big and strong and can run faster than anything. We like going out for a romp, it keeps us fit. I'll be just like her once I've had a bit of training – might need a nap first, though. Wonder if they'll let me drive the police car?

191

✔ *For my next trick, I will make you disappear …*

♪ *There – you're gone!*